Starfall
Sing-Along

Volume 2

A book of lyrics with audio CD.

Starfall®

Starfall Education
P.O. Box 359, Boulder, CO 80306

Table of Contents

1 Aa /a/ Alligator

Aa /a/ alligator
Bb /b/ ball
Cc /k/ computer
Dd /d/ doll
Ee /e/ elephant
Ff /f/ fingers
Gg /g/ gumballs
Hh /h/ helicopter
Ii /i/ itchy
Jj /j/ jump
Kk /k/ keys
Ll /l/ lollipop
Mm /m/ monkey
Nn /n/ no
Oo /o/ octopus
Pp /p/ pizza
Qq /qu/ queen
Rr /r/ rain
Ss /s/ snake
Tt /t/ tiger
Uu /u/ up
Vv /v/ vacuum
Ww /w/ window
Xx /x/ ox
Yy /y/ yawn
Zz /z/ zipper
Now I know my ABCs.

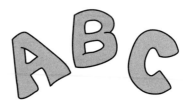

There was a man lived in the moon,
lived in the moon, lived in the moon,
there was a man lived in the moon,
and his name was Aiken Drum.

He played upon a ladle,
a ladle, a ladle,
he played upon a ladle,
and his name was Aiken Drum.

His hat was made of Swiss cheese,
of Swiss cheese, of Swiss cheese,
his hat was made of Swiss cheese,
and his name was Aiken Drum.

He coat was made of spinach,
of spinach, of spinach,
his coat was made of spinach,
and his name was Aiken Drum.

His buttons were made of popcorn,
of popcorn, of popcorn,
his buttons were made of popcorn,
and his name was Aiken Drum.

He played upon a ladle,
a ladle, a ladle,
he played upon a ladle,
and his name was Aiken Drum.

His hair was made of spaghetti,
spaghetti, spaghetti,
his hair was made of spaghetti,
and his name was Aiken Drum.

3 **Are You Sleeping?** (Frère Jacques)

Are you sleeping, are you sleeping,
Brother John, Brother John?

Morning bells are ringing, morning bells are ringing,
Ding, ding, dong. Ding, ding, dong.

(repeat)

4 **Autumn Leaves**

"Come, little leaves," said the wind one day.
"Come over the meadow with me to play;
Put on your dresses of red and gold,
Winter is coming, and the days grow cold."

Soon as the leaves heard the loud wind call,
Down they came, fluttering, one and all;
Over the green meadow they danced and flew,
Singing the soft little songs they knew.

Johnny had a little dog,
And Bingo was his name-O.
B-I-N-G-O!
B-I-N-G-O!
B-I-N-G-O!
And Bingo was his name-O!

Johnny had a little dog,
And Bingo was his name-O.
(Clap)-I-N-G-O!
(Clap)-I-N-G-O!
(Clap)-I-N-G-O!
And Bingo was his name-O!

Johnny had a little dog,
And Bingo was his name-O.
(Clap, Clap)-N-G-O!
(Clap, Clap)-N-G-O!
(Clap, Clap)-N-G-O!
And Bingo was his name-O!

Johnny had a little dog,
And Bingo was his name-O.
(Clap, Clap, Clap)-G-O!
(Clap, Clap, Clap)-G-O!
(Clap, Clap, Clap)-G-O!
And Bingo was his name-O!

Johnny had a little dog,
And Bingo was his name-O.
(Clap, Clap, Clap, Clap)-O!
(Clap, Clap, Clap, Clap)-O!
(Clap, Clap, Clap, Clap)-O!
And Bingo was his name-O!

Johnny had a little dog,
And Bingo was his name-O.
(Clap, Clap, Clap, Clap, Clap)
(Clap, Clap, Clap, Clap, Clap)
(Clap, Clap, Clap, Clap, Clap)
And Bingo was his name-O!

6 Coming Round the Mountain

She'll be coming round the mountain when she comes (toot toot)
She'll be coming round the mountain when she comes (toot toot)
She'll be coming round the mountain
She'll be coming round the mountain
She'll be coming round the mountain when she comes
        (toot toot)

She'll be driving six white horses when she comes (whoa back)
She'll be driving six white horses when she comes (whoa back)
She'll be driving six white horses
She'll be driving six white horses
She'll be driving six white horses when she comes
        (whoa back, toot toot)

Oh, we'll all go out to meet her when she comes (Hi Babe)
Oh, we'll all go out to meet her when she comes (Hi Babe)
Oh, we'll all go out to meet her
Oh, we'll all go out to meet her
Oh, we'll all go out to meet her when she comes
        (Hi Babe, whoa back, toot toot)

She'll be wearing red pajamas when she comes (scratch scratch)
She'll be wearing red pajamas when she comes (scratch scratch)
She'll be wearing red pajamas
She'll be wearing red pajamas
She'll be wearing red pajamas when she comes
        (scratch scratch, Hi Babe, whoa back, toot toot)

She will have to sleep with Grandma when she comes (snore snore)
She will have to sleep with Grandma when she comes (snore snore)
She will have to sleep with Grandma
She will have to sleep with Grandma
She will have to sleep with Grandma when she comes
        (snore snore, scratch scratch, Hi Babe, whoa back, toot toot)

Day and Night 7

Tune: Three Blind Mice

The earth spins
The earth spins
See how it goes
See how it goes
To watch it spin is quite a sight
This is why we have day and night
Round and round with all its might
The earth spins
The earth spins

Dinosaur Dance 8

It's Dinosaur Dance.
Come hop, skip, jump, and prance.
T-Rex, Long Neck, and you.
Trees, leaves, and flowers, too.
So, wiggle your fingers and nose,
And shake your feet and toes.
Let's hop, skip, jump, and prance.
It's the Dinosaur Dance!

9 Down by the Bay

Down by the bay where the watermelons grow,
Back to my home I dare not go.
For if I do my mother will say,
"Did you ever see a pig dancing a jig?"
Down by the bay.

Down by the bay where the watermelons grow,
Back to my home I dare not go.
For if I do my mother will say,
"Did you ever see a fox pulling an ox?"
Down by the bay.

Down by the bay where the watermelons grow,
Back to my home I dare not go.
For if I do my mother will say,
"Did you ever see a bear wearing underwear?"
Down by the bay.

Down by the bay where the watermelons grow,
Back to my home I dare not go.
For if I do my mother will say,
"Did you ever see a cow taking a bow?"
Down by the bay.

Down by the bay where the watermelons grow,
Back to my home I dare not go.
For if I do my mother will say,
"Did you ever see a snake baking a cake?"
Down by the bay.

Down by the bay where the watermelons grow,
Back to my home I dare not go.
For if I do my mother will say,
"Did you ever see a frog walking a dog?"
Down by the bay.

Down by the bay where the watermelons grow,
Back to my home I dare not go.
For if I do my mother will say,
"Did you ever see a goat driving a boat?"
Down by the bay.

Five Little Bees

Tune: One Little Elephant Went Out to Play

One little bee was on a flower blue
Along came another and that made two.
Two little bees worked hard as can be
Along came another and now there are three.
Three little bees looked for flowers more
Along came another and now there are four.
Four little bees flew back to their hive
Along came another and now there are five
Five little bees met with all their friends
And that is how our poem ends!

Five Little Farmers

Five little farmers woke up with the sun
For it was early morning and chores were to be done
The first little farmer went to milk the cow
The second little farmer thought he'd better plow
The third little farmer fed the hungry hens
The fourth little farmer mended broken pens
The fifth little farmer took his vegetables to town
Baskets filled with cabbages and sweet potatoes brown
And when the work was finished
And the Western sky was red
Five little farmers tumbled into bed
(Ahhhhh...)

12 Five Little Speckled Frogs

Five little speckled frogs
Sat on a speckled log
Eating some most delicious bugs (yum yum)
One jumped into the pool
Where it was nice and cool
Then there were four green speckled frogs (glub glub)

        Four little speckled frogs
        Sat on a speckled log
        Eating some most delicious bugs (yum yum)
        One jumped into the pool
        Where it was nice and cool
        Then there were three green speckled frogs (glub glub)

Three little speckled frogs
Sat on a speckled log
Eating some most delicious bugs (yum yum)
One jumped into the pool
Where it was nice and cool
Then there were two green speckled frogs (glub glub)

        Two little speckled frogs
        Sat on a speckled log
        Eating some most delicious bugs (yum yum)
        One jumped into the pool
        Where it was nice and cool
        Then there was one green speckled frog (glub glub)

One little speckled frog
Sat on a speckled log
Eating some most delicious bugs (yum yum)
One jumped into the pool
Where it was nice and cool
Then there were no green speckled frogs (glub glub)

Five Little Teddy Bears

Chant: rap

Five little teddy bears dancing on the floor,
One fell down and then there were four.

      Four little teddy bears climbing up a tree,
      One found a beehive and then there were three.

Three little teddy bears wondering what to do,
One chased a bunny rabbit, then there were two.

      Two little teddy bears looking for some fun.
      One took a swim and that left one.

One little teddy bear sitting all alone,
He looked all around and then went home.

14 Going on a Forest Walk

Tune: Going on a Bear Hunt

Going on a forest walk
But I'm not afraid
Got my running shoes
And my camera by my side

I see a mouse hole...
Underneath that tree...
Stay still...
A mouse...
"May we take your picture, please?"

I hear hoot-hooting...
Way up in the tree...
Listen...
An owl...
"May we take your picture, please?"

I see a web...
Glistening in the sun...
Over there...
A spider...
"May we take your picture, please?"

I see a bird...
Flying in the sky...
Look up...
An eagle...
"May we take your picture, please?"

I see something slithering...
Along the forest floor...
Stay back...
A snake...
"May we take your picture, please?"

I see a cave...
Who lives in there?...
Careful...
It's a bear!!

Use those running shoes...
Run run run...
Whew! We're safe...
That was fun!

Happy and You Know It

If you're happy and you know it clap your hands. (clap clap)
If you're happy and you know it clap your hands. (clap clap)
If you're happy and you know it then your face should surely show it.
If you're happy and you know it clap your hands. (clap clap)

If you're happy and you know it stomp your feet. (stomp stomp)
If you're happy and you know it stomp your feet. (stomp stomp)
If you're happy and you know it then your face should surely show it.
If you're happy and you know it stomp your feet. (stomp stomp)

If you're happy and you know it shout "Hooray!" (Hoo-Ray!)
If you're happy and you know it shout "Hooray!" (Hoo-Ray!)
If you're happy and you know it then your face should surely show it.
If you're happy and you know it shout "Hooray!" (Hoo-Ray!)

If you're happy and you know it do all three. (clap stomp Hoo-Ray!)
If you're happy and you know it do all three. (clap stomp Hoo-Ray!)
If you're happy and you know it then your face should surely show it.
If you're happy and you know it do all three. (clap stomp Hoo-Ray!)
That's all!

16 If All the Raindrops

If all the raindrops
Were lemon drops and gumdrops
Oh, what a rain that would be!
Standing outside, with my mouth open wide
Ah, ah, ah, ah, ah, ah, ah, ah, ah, ah
Ah, ah, ah, ah, ah, ah, ah, ah, ah, ah
If all the raindrops
Were lemon drops and gumdrops
Oh, what a rain that would be!

    If all the snowflakes
    Were candy bars and milkshakes
    Oh, what a snow that would be!
    Standing outside, with my mouth open wide
    Ah, ah, ah, ah, ah, ah, ah, ah, ah, ah
    Ah, ah, ah, ah, ah, ah, ah, ah, ah, ah
    If all the snowflakes
    Were candy bars and milkshakes
    Oh, what a snow that would be!

If all the sunbeams
Were bubblegum and ice cream
Oh, what a sun that would be!
Standing outside, with my mouth open wide
Ah, ah, ah, ah, ah, ah, ah, ah, ah, ah
Ah, ah, ah, ah, ah, ah, ah, ah, ah, ah
If all the sunbeams
Were bubblegum and ice cream
Oh, what a sun that would be!

I'm a Little Teapot 17

I'm a little teapot
Short and stout
Here is my handle
Here is my spout

When I get all steamed up
Hear me shout
"Tip me over and pour me out!"

(repeat)

I've Been Working on the Railroad 18

I've been working on the railroad
All the live-long day.
I've been working on the railroad
Just to pass the time away.
Don't you hear the whistle blowing,
Rise up so early in the morn;
Don't you hear the captain shouting,
"Dinah, blow your horn!"
> Dinah, won't you blow,
> Dinah, won't you blow,
> Dinah, won't you blow your horn?
> Dinah, won't you blow,
> Dinah, won't you blow,
> Dinah, won't you blow your horn?
Someone's in the kitchen with Dinah
Someone's in the kitchen I know
Someone's in the kitchen with Dinah
Strummin' on the old banjo!
And singin' fee, fie, fiddly-i-o
Fee, fie, fiddly-i-o-o-o-o
Fee, fie, fiddly-i-o
Strummin' on the old banjo.

19 Jimmy Crack Corn

Jimmy crack corn, and I don't care
Jimmy crack corn, and I don't care
Jimmy crack corn, and I don't care
Today's your birthday

    Right hand up, and I don't care
    Right hand up, and I don't care
    Right hand up, and I don't care
    Now let's all stand still

Left hand up, and I don't care
Left hand up, and I don't care
Left hand up, and I don't care
Now let's all stand still

    Both hands up, and I don't care
    Both hands up, and I don't care
    Both hands up, and I don't care
    Circle round and round

20 John Jacob Jingleheimer Schmidt

John Jacob Jingleheimer Schmidt,
His name is my name too.
Whenever I go out, the people always shout,
There goes John Jacob Jingleheimer Schmidt,
Tra la la la la la la!

(repeat)

Tune: London Bridge

We stay healthy, yes we do
yes we do, yes we do
We stay healthy, yes we do
all year long.

We eat lots of healthy food
healthy food, healthy food
We eat lots of healthy food
all year long.

We brush our teeth and comb our hair
comb our hair, comb our hair
We brush our teeth and comb our hair
all year long.

We like all kinds of exercise
exercise, exercise
We like all kinds of exercise
all year long.

So healthy kids we'll always be
always be, always be
Healthy kids we'll always be
all year long!

Little Jack Pumpkin Face **22**

Little Jack Pumpkin Face
Lived on a vine,
Little Jack Pumpkin Face
Thought it was fine.
First he was small and green,
Then big and yellow,
Little Jack Pumpkin Face
Is a fine fellow.

23 Little Red Caboose

Little red caboose (chug chug chug)
Little red caboose (chug chug)
Little red caboose behind the train

Smoke stack on its back (back back back)
Comin' down the track (track track track)
Little red caboose behind the train

(repeat)
(whoo hoo!)

24 London Bridge

London Bridge is falling down,
Falling down, Falling down.
London Bridge is falling down,
My fair lady.

Build it up with wood and clay,
Wood and clay, Wood and clay.
Build it up with wood and clay,
My fair lady.

Wood and clay will wash away,
Wash away, Wash away.
Wood and clay will wash away,
My fair lady.

Build it up with iron bars
Iron bars, Iron bars.
Build it up with iron bars,
My fair lady.

Iron bars will bend and break,
Bend and break, Bend and break.
Iron bars will bend and break,
My fair lady.

Build it up with stone so strong,
Stone so strong, Stone so strong.
Build it up with stone so strong,
My fair lady.

Stone so strong will last so long,
Last so long, Last so long.
Stone so strong will last so long,
My fair lady.

Mix a Pancake

Mix a pancake,
Stir a pancake,
Pop it in the pan;
Fry the pancake,
Toss the pancake,
Catch it if you can.

(repeat)

Months of the Year

52 weeks make a year
(52 weeks make a year)
Soon a new one will be here
(Soon we'll see another year)

12 months also make a year
(There are 12 months in a year)
Please repeat them loud and clear
(We'll repeat them when we hear)
January (January)
February (February)
March, April, May (March, April, May)
June, July, and August (June, July, and August)

Four more on the way
(Four more left to say)

September (September)
October (October)
November (November)
December (December)

Now we know them, have no fear
There are 12 months in every year

27 Muffin Man

Do you know the muffin man,
The muffin man, the muffin man,
Do you know the muffin man,
Who lives on Starfall Lane?
Yes, I know the muffin man,
The muffin man, the muffin man,
Yes, I know the muffin man,
Who lives on Starfall Lane.

28 Oceans

Tune: BINGO

The oceans are just full of life
let's see what we can see-ee,
dol-phins, whales, and squid,
dol-phins, whales, and squid,
dol-phins, whales, and squid
all live in the sea.

The oceans are just full of life
let's see what we can see-ee
star-fish, sharks, and clams
star-fish, sharks, and clams
star-fish, sharks, and clams
all live in the sea.

The oceans are just full of life
let's see what we can see-ee
lob-sters, seals, and shrimp
lob-sters, seals, and shrimp
lob-sters, seals, and shrimp
all live in the sea.

The oceans are just full of life
but NOT for you and me-ee
not for you and me
not for you and me
not for you and me
we don't live in the sea!

One Little Elephant Went Out to Play

One little elephant went out to play
Upon a spider's web one day;
She had such enormous fun,
She asked another little elephant to come!

Two little elephants went out to play
Upon a spider's web one day;
They had such enormous fun,
They asked another little elephant to come!

Three little elephants went out to play
Upon a spider's web one day;
They had such enormous fun,
They asked another little elephant to come!

Four little elephants went out to play
Upon a spider's web one day;
They had such enormous fun,
They asked another little elephant to come!

Five little elephants went out to play
Upon a spider's web one day;
They had such enormous fun,
They didn't ask another little elephant to come!

30 One Potato

One potato, two potato
Three potato, four,
Five potato, six potato
Seven potato, more!

Eight potato, nine potato,
Ten potatoes please
Jump up, turn around
Then touch your knees!

(repeat)

31 Parts of My Body
Tune: (Twinkle, Twinkle, Little Star)

Little feet can make you go
Little arms swing to and fro
Little ears can make you hear
Loving words of mother dear
Little nose is useful, too
Little eyes play peek-a-boo
Little tongue can make you say
Happy words in work and play
All together we will do
Things for me and things for you

Plane Ride

Tune: Wheels on the Bus

The wheels on the plane go round and round,
round and round, round and round.
The wheels on the plane go round and round,
all along the ground.

The captain on the plane says, "Buckle up now!"
"Buckle up now!" "Buckle up now!"
The captain on the plane says, "Buckle up now!
We'll show you how."

The engine on the plane takes you up so high,
up so high, up so high.
The engine on the plane takes you up so high
as we soar through the sky.

The crew on the plane brings drinks and a treat,
drinks and a treat, drinks and a treat.
The crew on the plane brings drinks and a treat,
now it's time to eat.

The control tower says, "The runway's clear!"
"The runway's clear!" "The runway's clear!"
The control tower says, "The runway's clear,
you can land here."

The journey on the plane is over now,
over now, over now.
The journey on the plane is over now,
what fun! WOW!

33 Pop Goes the Weasel

All around the mulberry bush,
The monkey chased the weasel.
The monkey thought 'twas all in fun,
Pop! goes the weasel.

I've no time to wait or sigh,
No patience to wait till by and by,
Kiss me quick, I'm off, goodbye!
Pop! goes the weasel.

34 Shoo Fly

Shoo, fly, don't bother me,
Shoo, fly, don't bother me,
Shoo, fly, don't bother me,
For I belong to somebody.
I feel, I feel,
I feel like a morning star,
I feel, I feel,
I feel like a morning star.
I feel, I feel,
I feel like a morning star,
I feel, I feel,
I feel like a morning star.
Shoo, fly, don't bother me,
Shoo, fly, don't bother me,
Shoo, fly, don't bother me,
For I belong… I belong… I belong to somebody.
(Thank you very much!)

Six Little Ducks

Six little ducks
That I once knew
Fat ones, skinny ones
Fair ones, too
But the one little duck
With the feather on his back
He led the others
With a quack, quack, quack

Quack, quack, quack
Quack, quack, quack
He led the others
With a quack, quack, quack

Down to the river
They would go
Wibble, wobble, wibble, wobble
To and fro
But the one little duck
With the feather on his back
He led the others
With a quack, quack, quack

Quack, quack, quack
Quack, quack, quack
He led the others
With a quack, quack, quack

Back from the river
They would come
Wibble, wobble, wibble, wobble
Ho, hum, hum
But the one little duck
With the feather on his back
He led the others
With a quack, quack, quack

Quack, quack, quack
Quack, quack, quack
He led the others
With a quack, quack, quack

36 Skip to My Lou

Fly's in the buttermilk,
Shoo, fly, shoo,
Fly's in the buttermilk,
Shoo, fly, shoo,
Fly's in the buttermilk,
Shoo, fly, shoo,
Skip to my Lou, my darling.
Skip, skip, skip to my Lou
Skip, skip, skip to my Lou
Skip, skip, skip to my Lou
Skip to my Lou, my darling!

37 Teddy Bear, Teddy Bear, Turn Around

Teddy bear, teddy bear,
Turn around.
Teddy bear, teddy bear,
Touch the ground.
Teddy bear, teddy bear,
Reach up high.
Teddy bear, teddy bear,
Wink one eye.

Teddy bear, teddy bear,
Dance on toes.
Teddy bear, teddy bear,
Touch your nose.
Teddy bear, teddy bear,
Slap your knees.
Teddy bear, teddy bear,
Sit down please.

Ten Bears in the Bed

Ten bears in the bed
And the little one said
"I'm crowded, roll over"
So they all rolled over
And one fell out

Nine bears in the bed
And the little one said
"I'm crowded, roll over"
So they all rolled over
And one fell out

Eight bears in the bed
And the little one said
"I'm crowded, roll over"
So they all rolled over
And one fell out

Seven bears in the bed
And the little one said
"I'm crowded, roll over"
So they all rolled over
And one fell out

Six bears in the bed
And the little one said
"I'm crowded, roll over"
So they all rolled over
And one fell out

Five bears in the bed
And the little one said
"I'd crowded, roll over"
So they all rolled over
And one fell out

Four bears in the bed
And the little one said
"I'm crowded, roll over"
So they all rolled over
And one fell out

Three bears in the bed
And the little one said
"I'm crowded, roll over"
So they all rolled over
And one fell out

Two bears in the bed
And the little one said
"I'm crowded, roll over"
So they all rolled over
And one fell out

One bear in the bed
And the little one said
"Good night!"

39   Ten Little Monkeys

Ten little monkeys going out to dine.
One got full and then there were nine.

Nine little monkeys stuck in a gate.
One cried out and then there were eight.

Eight little monkeys slept until eleven.
One overslept and then there were seven.

Seven little monkeys stopped to pick up sticks.
One was left behind and then there were six.

Six little monkeys playing by a hive.
A bumblebee chased one, then there were five.

Five little monkeys went through a door.
One got lost and then there were four.

Four little monkeys going out to sea.
One went swimming and then there were three.

Three little monkeys walking in the zoo.
One went to play and then there were two.

Two little monkeys sitting in the sun.
One got sunburned, then there was one.

One little monkey with his little wife.
Lived all his days a happy little life.

The ants go marching **one by one**, hurrah, hurrah
The ants go marching one by one, hurrah, hurrah
The ants go marching one by one
The little one stops to **suck his thumb**

And they all go marching down to the ground
To get out of the rain, BOOM! BOOM! BOOM!

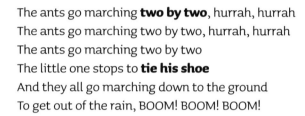

The ants go marching **two by two**, hurrah, hurrah
The ants go marching two by two, hurrah, hurrah
The ants go marching two by two
The little one stops to **tie his shoe**
And they all go marching down to the ground
To get out of the rain, BOOM! BOOM! BOOM!

The ants go marching **three by three**, hurrah, hurrah
The ants go marching three by three, hurrah, hurrah
The ants go marching three by three
The little one stops to **ride a bee**
And they all go marching down to the ground
To get out of the rain, BOOM! BOOM! BOOM!

The ants go marching **four by four**, hurrah, hurrah
The ants go marching four by four, hurrah, hurrah
The ants go marching four by four
The little one stops to **ask for more**
And they all go marching down to the ground
To get out of the rain, BOOM! BOOM! BOOM!

The ants go marching **five by five**, hurrah, hurrah
The ants go marching five by five, hurrah, hurrah
The ants go marching five by five
The little one stops to **jump and to dive**
And they all go marching down to the ground
To get out of the rain, BOOM! BOOM! BOOM!

(continued...)

The ants go marching **six by six**, hurrah, hurrah
The ants go marching six by six, hurrah, hurrah
The ants go marching six by six
The little one stops to **pick up sticks**
And they all go marching down to the ground
To get out of the rain, BOOM! BOOM! BOOM!

The ants go marching **seven by seven**, hurrah, hurrah
The ants go marching seven by seven, hurrah, hurrah
The ants go marching seven by seven
The little one stops to **write with a pen**
And they all go marching down to the ground
To get out of the rain, BOOM! BOOM! BOOM!

The ants go marching **eight by eight**, hurrah, hurrah
The ants go marching eight by eight, hurrah, hurrah
The ants go marching eight by eight
The little one stops to **rollerskate**
And they all go marching down to the ground
To get out of the rain, BOOM! BOOM! BOOM!

The ants go marching **nine by nine**, hurrah, hurrah
The ants go marching nine by nine, hurrah, hurrah
The ants go marching nine by nine
The little one stops to **drink and dine**
And they all go marching down to the ground
To get out of the rain, BOOM! BOOM! BOOM!

The ants go marching **ten by ten**, hurrah, hurrah
The ants go marching ten by ten, hurrah, hurrah
The ants go marching ten by ten
The little one stops to shout **"The End!"**
And they all go marching down to the ground
To get out of the rain, BOOM! BOOM! BOOM! BOOM!

The Bear Went Over the Mountain **41**

The bear went over the mountain,
The bear went over the mountain,
The bear went over the mountain,
To see what he could see.
And all that he could see,
And all that he could see,
Was the other side of the mountain,
The other side of the mountain,
The other side of the mountain,
Was all that he could see!

The Falling Star **42**

I saw a star slide down the sky
Blinding the north wind as it went by
Too burning and too quick to hold
Too lovely to be bought or sold
Only good to make wishes on
            Starlight, Starbright
            First star I see tonight
            I wish I may, I wish I might
            Have the wish I wish tonight
And then forever to be gone.

43 The Gingerbread Boy

Hey, hey, Gingerbread Boy,
Hey, hey, Gingerbread Boy!

The Gingerbread Boy is here today,
To join us in our work and play.

Hey, hey, Gingerbread Boy,
Hey, hey, Gingerbread Boy!

The ABCs he wants to learn.
He's so polite and waits his turn.

Hey, hey, Gingerbread Boy,
Hey, hey, Gingerbread Boy!

"Please" and "thank you" we hear him say
Each and every single day.

Hey, hey, Gingerbread Boy,
Hey, hey, Gingerbread Boy!

He loves to run and shouts with glee,
"I'm the Gingerbread Boy, you can't catch me!"

Hey, hey, Gingerbread Boy,
Hey, hey, Gingerbread Boy!

Hooray, hooray, hooray, hooray,
The Gingerbread Boy is here to stay!

Hooray, hooray, hooray, hooray,
The Gingerbread Boy is here to stay!

The Goodbye Song 44

Tune: If You're Happy and You Know It
(bolded words are stressed)

If you **had** a happy day, clap your hands.
If you had a happy day, clap your hands.
If you had a happy day, if you had a happy day,
If you had a happy day, clap your hands!

If **you** had fun today, stomp your feet…

If you made a new friend, say hooray…

The Little Turtle 45

There was a little turtle.
He lived in a box.
He swam in a puddle.
He climbed on the rocks.

He snapped at a mosquito.
He snapped at a flea.
He snapped at a minnow.
And he snapped at me.

He caught the mosquito.
He caught the flea.
He caught the minnow.
But he didn't catch me.

The More We Get Together 46

The more we get together, together, together
The more we get together, the happier we'll be
'Cause your friends are my friends
And my friends are your friends
The more we get together the happier we'll be.
(repeat)

47 The Time Song

60 seconds make a minute
(60 seconds make a minute)
Something new you can learn in it
(We learn something every minute)

60 minutes make an hour
(60 minutes make an hour)
Work with all your might and power
(We will work with all our power)

24 hours make a day
(24 hours make a day)
Time enough for work and play
(Time for work and time for play)

7 days will make a week
(7 days will make a week)
Say them after as I speak
(We'll repeat them as you speak)

Monday (Monday)
Tuesday (Tuesday)
Wednesday (Wednesday)
Thursday (Thursday)
Friday (Friday)
Saturday (Saturday)
And the last is Sunday (Sunday)

7 days a week will make
(7 days a week will make)
We can learn if time we take

There's a Hole in the Bottom of the Sea

There's a hole, there's a hole, there's a hole in the bottom of the sea.

There's a log in the hole in the bottom of the sea. There's a log in the hole in the bottom of the sea. There's a hole, there's a hole, there's a hole in the bottom of the sea.

There's a bump on the log in the hole in the bottom of the sea. There's a bump on the log in the hole in the bottom of the sea. There's a hole, there's a hole, there's a hole in the bottom of the sea.

There's a frog on the bump on the log in the hole in the bottom of the sea. There's a frog on the bump on the log in the hole in the bottom of the sea. There's a hole, there's a hole, there's a hole in the bottom of the sea.

There's a tail on the frog on the bump on the log in the hole in the bottom of the sea. There's a tail on the frog on the bump on the log in the hole in the bottom of the sea. There's a hole, there's a hole, there's a hole in the bottom of the sea.

There's a speck on the tail on the frog on the bump on the log in the hole in the bottom of the sea. There's a speck on the tail on the frog on the bump on the log in the hole in the bottom of the sea. There's a hole, there's a hole, there's a hole in the bottom of the sea. There's a hole, there's a hole, there's a hole in the bottom of the sea.

49 Where Is My Head?

Tune: Where Is Thumbkin?

Where is my head? (Where is my head?)
Here it is (Here it is)
Make a smile and not a frown (We can look both up and down)
Nod, nod, nod (Nod, nod, nod)

Where are my hands? (Where are my hands?)
Here they are (Here they are)
Clap your hands and make some noise (We are clever girls and boys)
Clap, clap, clap (Clap, clap, clap)

Where are my feet? (Where are my feet?)
Here they are (Here they are)
Use your feet to move around (We jump up and then sit down)
Stomp, stomp, stomp (Stomp, stomp, stomp)

Where Is Thumbkin? 50

Where is Thumbkin?
Where is Thumbkin?
Here I am!
Here I am!
How are you today, sir?
Very well, I thank you.
Run away.
Run away.

Where is Pointer?
Where is Pointer?
Here I am!
Here I am!
How are you today, sir?
Very well, I thank you.
Run away.
Run away.

Where is Middleman?
Where is Middleman?
Here I am!
Here I am!
How are you today, sir?
Very well, I thank you.
Run away.
Run away.

Where is Ringman?
Where is Ringman?
Here I am!
Here I am!
How are you today, sir?
Very well, I thank you.
Run away.
Run away.

Where is Pinkie?
Where is Pinkie?
Here I am!
Here I am!
How are you today, sir?
Very well, I thank you.
Run away.
Run away.

Where is the family?
Where is the family?
Here we are!
Here we are!
How you today, sir?
Very well, we thank you.
Run away.
Run away.

Yankee Doodle 51

Yankee Doodle went to town
A-riding on a pony
Stuck a feather in his hat
And called it macaroni.
Yankee Doodle, keep it up
Yankee Doodle dandy
Mind the music and the step
And with the girls be handy.

52 Yonder in the Pair, Pair Patch

Tune: Paw, Paw Patch

Where oh where can we find a pair?
Where oh where can we find a pair?
Where oh where can we find a pair?
Way down yonder in the Pair, Pair Patch!

Pick up mittens and put them in a basket
Pick up mittens and put them in a basket
Pick up mittens and put them in a basket
Way down yonder in the Pair, Pair Patch!

Pick up shoes, put them in the basket
Pick up shoes, put them in the basket
Pick up shoes, put them in the basket
Way down yonder in the Pair, Pair Patch!

Pick up skates, put them in a basket
Pick up skates, put them in a basket
Pick up skates, put them in a basket
Way down yonder in the Pair, Pair Patch!

Come on kids let's go find pairs
Come on kids let's go find pairs
Come on kids let's go find pairs
Way down yonder in the Pair, Pair Patch!

Where oh where can we find a pair?
Where oh where can we find a pair?
Where oh where can we find a pair?
Way down yonder in the Pair, Pair Patch!